Mud Kitchen Crafts

60 Awesome Ideas
FOR EPIC OUTDOOR PLAY

SOPHIE PICKLES, Creator of SophiePickles.com

PAGE STREET
PUBLISHING CO.

PAGE STREET
PUBLISHING CO.

First published in 2021 by
Page Street Publishing Co.
27 Congress Street, Suite 105
Salem, MA 01970
www.pagestreetpublishing.com

Distributed by Macmillan, sales in Canada by The Canadian Manda Group.

25 24 23 22 21   1 2 3 4 5

ISBN-13: 978-1-64567-275-3
ISBN-10: 1-64567-275-1

Library of Congress Control Number: 2020948808

Cover and book design by Kylie Alexander for Page Street Publishing Co.
Photography by Sophie Pickles

Printed and bound in China

Page Street Publishing protects our planet by donating to nonprofits like The Trustees, which focuses on local land conservation.

To Finley and Rupert,
whose love of mud never falters.

Contents

Introduction

As an early years expert, teacher and parent, I know this for certain: Young children are endlessly fascinated with nature and the great outdoors. They are never happier than when they are given the opportunity to explore and play with their natural surroundings. Mud play and mud kitchens are a large part of this, as well as being a beloved backyard activity in many homes across the world; the educational philosophy behind mud play is something that has been studied and researched at the highest level. Put simply, (most) children love mud, and creating a simple mud kitchen in your backyard is often one of the greatest gifts you can give them.

As the name suggests, mud kitchens typically involve playing with mud—but that is not their sole purpose. In fact, mud kitchen play can be done without any mud at all! It is the process of exploring, concocting, mixing and measuring that forms the basis of the mud kitchen philosophy, and this can be done using water, natural objects, sand and, yes, mud.

As a mom of two young mud-loving boys, we spend a lot of time outside. There's something about being out in the fresh air that has a positive effect on all of us. Tantrums are instantly forgotten and moans fade away as we all become absorbed in wonderful mud kitchen play. Out of all the activities we do at home (or even away from home), playing with the mud kitchen is the one thing that is guaranteed to elicit smiles and hold their attention for a prolonged period of time—something that I know will be as important to you as it is to me!

There are so many reasons why you should delve into the world of mud kitchens with your child. They are fantastically fun, will entertain for hours and provide amazing learning opportunities. In all honesty, when it comes to mud kitchen play and learning, there are too many educational opportunities to name. By exploring the activities in this book, your child will deepen their understanding of every area of learning, from math and problem-solving to creativity, language, art and science.

Not only will their brains grow, but their muscles will too! Mud kitchen play has numerous physical benefits, from developing arm and shoulder strength to fine motor skills for writing. If you would like to learn more about how you can enhance these physical opportunities, read on to learn about creating and setting up your own mud kitchen.

Sophie
x

Making a Mud Kitchen

Making a mud kitchen does not have to be expensive; in fact, it need not cost much of anything at all. It's easy to be tempted by expensive purpose-built mud kitchens that you see in stores and online, but the very best kitchens, and the ones that will be treasured most by your child, are the ones you create together.

YOUR MUD KITCHEN

Your physical mud kitchen structure can easily be made from a couple of wooden boards held up at either end by plastic crates or concrete blocks. Pallet boards also make perfect surfaces for play. Our mud kitchen, which you will see throughout this book, is an old TV unit that was made from scaffolding boards and was given to us by some friends. Of course, if you want to spend more money and buy a purpose-built mud kitchen, please don't let me put you off. Just know that it absolutely isn't necessary from a learning and enjoyment point of view.

Whichever route you choose to go, make sure there is ample flat workspace for your child. You may wish to provide this on two levels so that they can choose whether to sit or stand. Having some spare planks of wood resting up against a nearby wall will allow you to extend the work-space when necessary, as well as increase the flexibility of your space.

SETUP

More important than looks is where you choose to position the mud kitchen in your outdoor space. This is something that can make a huge difference, not only to the fun factor, but also to the educational benefits of engaging in mud kitchen play.

While it may seem useful to position your mud kitchen against a wall or fence, consider putting it in the middle of a space instead. Not only does this mean you can walk around it and easily access it from all angles, but it also helps to naturally promote conversation, language development and cooperative play. If you still prefer to lean your mud kitchen up against a vertical surface, or if you have limited space, consider introducing a small tree stump or circular station so that the opportunities to face each other and develop those conversational and sharing skills are still there.

Hanging up some of your utensils not only saves space and makes them more appealing to the child but also has brilliant physical benefits. Consider hanging items ever so slightly higher than your child can reach, encouraging them to fully stretch out their arms and maybe even stand on their tiptoes. This will help develop their sense of balance, their core stability and their hand-eye coordination.

WATER SOURCE

Make sure you give your child access to a water source to enhance their play. Ideally this will come in the form of an outdoor tap and a hose, or a rain barrel, but you could use some prefilled buckets of water with a jug nearby.

The most important point to note here is how far you place the water source from the mud kitchen. Contrary to what you may assume, placing the kitchen next to the water source is actually counterproductive. If you position the mud kitchen at a reasonable distance from the water, it will mean your child has to carry the water from one point to another. This is not only a brilliant exercise in problem-solving, but the physical act of carrying the water will build up strength in their shoulders, arms and upper body. Believe it or not, strength in these areas will actually help your child be a more confident writer, as well as helping them with sports and other tasks requiring coordination.

WHAT ELSE TO GET

Jan White, educational advisor and expert in outdoor play, puts it best when she says, "The best mud kitchens, and those that have the most atmosphere and character, are made from found, gathered and donated items—especially when these come from the children's own families. It's important not to spend much money—what matters to children is that these things come from the real human world, to combine with the stuff of the real natural world."

Using real items rather than toys will give your child a sense of importance, purpose and independence as they play. We know that children love to imitate the activities that we as adults carry out every day, so providing your child with real pans, spoons, teapots and cups will elevate their play experience—and cost you a lot less, too! If you don't already have things in your home you could repurpose, thrifting is the very best thing you can do and is my favorite way to source materials for play.

I'll give you a list of everything you will need with each activity, but all these activities will be even more fun to play in a well-stocked mud kitchen, where your child can bash and mash and spoon and dump.

Essentials

- Baking trays
- Jugs
- Mixing bowls
- Mud
- Muffin tin
- Natural ingredients (see page 13)
- Pans with lids
- Plastic crates or bins to store equipment (unless your mud kitchen has cupboards or lots of shelves)
- Plates, cups and saucers
- Potato masher
- Pots or jars with lids to store natural ingredients
- Slotted spoon

- Spatula
- Washing-up bowl
- Water
- Wooden and metal spoons

Extras

- Bowls of different materials: wood, plastic, metal, stone
- Chalk and chalk board
- Different size spoons and scoops
- Empty coffee cans (great for storing objects and for play too)
- French press
- Funnel
- Gardening tools
- Ice cream scoop
- Magnifying glass
- Measuring cups of different sizes
- Mortar and pestle
- Pipette
- Play trays, small and large
- Sand
- Sieve
- Silicone ice cube tray
- Silicone muffin cups
- Teapot
- Turkey baster
- Tweezers

COLLECTING NATURAL INGREDIENTS

You will see that natural ingredients and "loose parts" play a large part in this book. Not only are they free and easily accessible, but they make wonderful additions to play and allow children to really connect with and understand the nature that surrounds them. Natural loose parts are easy to collect from your own backyard or by taking a walk in a local park or forest area (where you should only take things that have already fallen to the ground). Store them in jars and containers and keep them next to the mud kitchen so that your child always has easy access for play.

Look for:

- Acorns
- Bark
- Branches with and without leaves
- Chestnuts (some can be toxic if ingested)
- Dried flowers
- Feathers
- Fresh flowers and petals
- Grass, fresh and dried
- Gravel
- Leaves
- Log slices
- Moss
- Pine cones
- River rocks and pebbles
- Sawdust
- Seed pods
- Seeds
- Shells
- Sticks, twigs and logs
- Straw

Before You Begin

You may be concerned that you can't participate in real mud play if you don't have access to natural soil and mud from your backyard. Not so! Mud is easy to make by mixing dirt and water together. Simply buy a bag of soil from your local garden center and mix some with water to create mud. Experiment with different ratios of dirt to water to find your perfect consistency.

A TASTE-SAFE ALTERNATIVE

Mud can be made for play in many different forms. Depending upon your situation or the age of your child, you may like to consider using taste-safe play mud, rather than the real deal.

I personally believe there is no replacement for the texture, feel and wonderful variation in natural mud. As long as hands are kept from mouths and washed thoroughly afterwards, there is no reason why real mud can't be used for play, even with very young children.

Taste-safe mud has its benefits too, of course, especially if you have a young baby at home who likes to put everything in their mouth. Here is a recipe for some super simple, taste-safe mud.

❮ *Taste-safe mud*

Mix ½ cup (63 g) of flour (any flour will do) with 2 tablespoons (11 g) of cocoa powder in a bucket or bin. Measure out 2 cups (480 ml) of water and add it to the flour and cocoa little by little, mixing until you reach the right muddy consistency. You may not need to use all the water.

Although some of the activities in this book are taste-safe, I do not recommend eating any of them—not even if you use the taste-safe mud recipe here.

ALLERGIES

Some products used in some of the activities may contain allergens that aggravate sensitive skin. Please do not participate in any activity or use any ingredient that you think your child may be allergic to.

KEEPING SAFE

The activities in this book are suitable for children of all ages. (There really is no upper limit on play, as I can attest to!) All the ideas are toddler-friendly and have been tried and tested with my own two-year-old, with my seven-month-old never far behind. I suggest you decide for yourself, however, whether each individual activity is suitable for your own child, based on their age, abilities and personal interests.

With any child, do not leave any sharp tools such as scissors, knives or cheese graters within reach. When using these tools during activities, provide guidance and close supervision. You may wish to place your hands over your child's as they learn how to use them, or to keep certain tools for adult use only.

Playing in the great outdoors always presents a certain element of risk, but as long as children are closely supervised, particularly when using small parts or foraging for natural elements, these measured risks will actually allow them to test limits, explore nature and expand learning and experiences.

All the activities in this book should be undertaken alongside or under the supervision of an adult. It keeps everyone safe, and playing alongside our children is proven to deepen learning experiences, bonding and fun!

Mud Kitchen Cooking

From classic mud pies to mud soup and everything in between, these mud kitchen recipes are designed to ignite your child's interest and provide opportunities for them to use their own imaginations to take the play wherever they wish. Although each activity has advice on how to play, my greatest advice would be to follow your child's lead. If the mud soup suddenly becomes a magic potion, go with it!

Mud Pizza

This is an alternative take on the traditional mud pie. Mud pizzas will allow your child to unleash their creativity as they decorate with natural materials, as well as develop their mathematical knowledge as they experiment with the idea of simple measurements and patterns. (Remember to supervise children so they do not accidentally consume their mud pizza or its toppings.)

Supplies

Natural loose parts: leaves, petals, acorns, pine cones, pebbles, grass, etc.

Bowls or pots to hold your loose parts

Mud

Sand

Water

Measuring cups (optional)

Spreading knife

Spatula

Plates, for serving

How to Play

Collect some natural loose parts to act as toppings. Sort them into bowls or pots and set them to one side.

Add the mud, sand and water to a large bowl and get mixing! A few scoops of mud, a sprinkle of sand and a couple of cups of water—or let the children make up their own measurements. Add an extra element of challenge by asking your child to measure out set amounts of each of the ingredients.

Tip out your mixture onto a flat surface and pat it flat. Mold the sides until you have made a circle.

Now it's time to add the toppings. Why not suggest that your child make a pattern on the top of their mud pizza? This will encourage great math, art and problem-solving skills.

Divide into slices and share.

Potion Making

I have such happy memories of wandering around our garden as a child, gathering seeds and flower petals and crushing, mixing and swirling them to make my own magic potions. This is the perfect activity for budding scientists, lovers of magic and fantasy and children who just love to combine and create.

Supplies

Gathered foliage: petals, leaves, etc.

Food coloring

Bottles and jars

Water

Bowls, spoons and pans of different sizes

Scissors

Ladle

Mortar and pestle

How to Play

Before you begin potion making, go on a hunt around your garden, looking for foliage to add to your special brew. Use this opportunity to talk about things that are safe to use and things to leave untouched (think berries and the like). It is also the perfect opportunity to introduce the names of different plants and flowers. If you aren't sure yourself, grab a book or your phone and look them up together.

Add a few drops of food coloring to the bottles and fill them with water, giving each mixture a stir if necessary.

Lay out the bottles containing the colored water in your mud kitchen area, along with some bowls, spoons and pans. This invitation to play will encourage your child to begin potion making.

Using scissors to cut the leaves and petals down to size will develop hand strength and coordination, while the pouring, mixing and grinding in a mortar and pestle will improve accuracy and gross motor skills.

Add a little imagination and creative play and discuss what the magic potion will be used for. What magical powers will it instill?

Children may even like to write down their recipe so that they can use it again next time.

Perfume Shop

This is a classic mud kitchen activity for spring and summer days. Create a collection of perfumes and then use them to make a shop. Not only will the perfume creation inspire creativity and motor skills, but the idea of a shop will encourage imaginative play and develop math skills.

Supplies

Gathered petals and flowers

Scissors

Mortar and pestle

Mixing bowl or saucepan

Jug

Water

Wooden and metal spoons

Food coloring (optional)

Essential oils (optional)

Slotted spoon or ladle

Sieve

Funnel

Pipettes or a turkey baster

Bottles with lids

Spray bottles (optional)

FOR THE SHOP

Sticky labels

Paper

Pencils

Coins

Carrier bags or baskets

How to Play

Cut the flowers and petals into different shapes and sizes, or grind them in the mortar and pestle. Add the petals and flowers to the mixing bowl and combine with water to make your perfume. Allow your child to experiment with adding food coloring or essential oils (with supervision) to create different scents and mixtures.

When the perfume is ready, use the spoon or ladle to decant it into bottles (used water bottles or even spray bottles are perfect for this), using a funnel or pipette to improve accuracy.

Help your child create labels for the perfume and stick them on the bottles, along with price tags. Now they are ready for their first customer. Role playing in this way is a fantastic tool for developing language, communication skills and creativity, not to mention all that mathematical skill-building, too.

NOTE: Save bunches of flowers from around your house when they have gone past their prime.

Mud Pies

I couldn't write a book about mud kitchens without including the humble mud pie. Whether it's a lump of mud slapped onto the sidewalk and left to bake in the sun, or a delicate beauty carefully measured, mixed and adorned with leaves and pine cones, the mud pie and its construction is a rite of passage for any mini mud chef.

Supplies

Mixing bowl

Mud

Sand

Water

Natural loose parts: small sticks, leaves, petals, acorns, pine cones, pebbles, grass, etc.

Bowls or pots, to hold your loose parts

Wooden and metal spoons

Measuring cups

Baking trays

Muffin tin or silicone cupcake cups

Spatula

Potato masher

Jug

Plates, cups and saucers

Scoops, spoons, pots, containers for play

How to Play

The beauty of mud pie making is that there are no rules to follow and imagination really can lead the way. If you would like some ideas for creating wonderful mud pies, however, or tips on facilitating deeper level play and learning, then read on.

Add the ingredients to a bowl—this could be a mixture of mud, sand, water, loose parts—and mix together. Enhance the learning by asking your child to select a certain quantity of ingredients to add to their bowl. For example, say, "We need to add five pebbles to our mixture. Let's count them out: one, two, three, four, five." Or, "Could you measure out 2 cups of mud?"

Divide the mixture into a muffin tin, silicone cupcake cups or even just onto the patio or sidewalk.

Look through your natural loose parts (or collect some if you don't have a supply) and use them to decorate the pies. This is the point where your child can let their imagination go wild. Why don't you decorate your own mud pies alongside them and narrate what you are choosing and where you are putting it. This will subtly encourage conversation and language development.

Leave your mud pies out in the sun to dry and observe how they change. Or just tip them all back into the bowl and start again.

Mud Dough

Let your little one put on their chef's hat and use the mud kitchen to create real mud dough. It's great for role-playing or creating dough shapes or sculptures. This activity will help build mathematical understanding, as well as present the physical challenge of pouring, mixing and kneading—all important precursors to writing.

Supplies

2 cups (250 g) flour

½ cup (146 g) salt

2 tbsp (20 g) cream of tartar

2 tbsp (30 ml) vegetable oil, baby oil or coconut oil

Mixing bowl

Pan

Brown food coloring

1½ cups (360 ml) boiling water

Dry compost or play sand

How to Make It

Make the playdough base by stirring together the flour, salt, cream of tartar and oil in a bowl until they're combined.

In a separate pan, add a few drops of food coloring to the boiling water until it reaches your desired color. Add the water to the dry ingredients and combine.

Allow the mixture to cool, then take it out of the bowl and knead for several minutes until it is no longer sticky.

Add some of the compost to the dough and knead it in, adjusting the amount to your liking. If the mixture is still sticky, you may want to add a little more compost.

Once you have tried the recipe together a few times, why not let your little one take the reins and make it for themselves? This will encourage independent thinking as well as further build on those math skills. Just make sure you handle the boiling water yourself.

> NOTE: Nothing is more fun than making *real* mud dough. However, using compost will mean your dough should not be kept for longer than a week. Please ensure your children do not put the dough near to or in their mouths. If you do not feel comfortable using compost, dry play sand is a great alternative and works just as well.

Mud Cookies

These mud cookies look almost good enough to eat. If you don't have time to make the mud dough, why not just use mud or clay from the garden instead?

....

Supplies

Rolling pin

Mud Dough (page 26)

Cookie cutters

Baking sheet

Natural loose parts: herbs, seeds, etc.

How to Play

Roll out the Mud Dough and use the cookie cutters to make and cut out cookie shapes.

Place each cookie onto the baking sheet and decorate it with the natural loose parts. You could use rosemary sprinkles, sunflower seed chocolate chips . . . imaginations really can run wild.

"Bake" in the mud kitchen oven until you're ready to serve, and pretend to eat.

Mud Soup

Making mud soup is a lesson in motor development, hand and shoulder
strength and creativity. There's something incredibly satisfying about
ripping, snipping, grinding and tearing ingredients and throwing them into
the pot—like cooking without the pressure of wondering how it will turn out.
The beauty of mud soup, as with all mud kitchen cooking,
is that it always turns out exactly as it's meant to.

Supplies

Dry dirt (soil or compost)

Pan

Natural loose parts: leaves,
petals, acorns, grass, etc.

Mortar and pestle

Herbs from your garden (see
page 45 for more information on
creating an herb garden for play)

Scissors

Water

Large wooden spoon

Ladle

Jug

Serving bowls or cups

How to Play

Add several scoops of dirt to a pan and throw in a selection of your
gathered ingredients. If you have a mortar and pestle, your child
may enjoy grinding some of the natural loose parts before adding
them to the mixture.

If you have an herb garden (see page 45), then adding in herbs and
either cutting them with scissors or tearing them with hands are
both great fine motor practices and also a wonderful sensory
experience, especially if you have managed to grow or gather
fragrant plants such as rosemary or lavender.

Collect and carry some water to the pan and fill it up.

Stir your scented concoction and ladle it into bowls or cups using a
ladle or by scooping out by the jugful and pouring them in.

Leaf Kebabs

There is beauty in the simplicity of the humble leaf kebab. It's a brilliant activity to choose if you would like to spend a little time focusing on hand-eye coordination, accuracy and math skills. I find that it's almost a meditative activity—perfect for a quiet afternoon.

Supplies

Leaves

Large flower heads

Thin sticks for kebab skewers

How to Play

Gather a selection of leaves, bearing in mind that any that are too brittle may be too delicate to put on the skewer. You may also want to gather some large flower heads (any bouquets that are now past their best would work really well here).

Take a thin stick, making sure it is sharp enough at one end, and carefully thread on the leaves and flower heads.

This often provides the perfect opportunity to talk about creating patterns. You may want to encourage your child to think about which leaves and flower heads they choose to put on at which point, so that they can create a simple repeating pattern.

Feed the Birds

Surely there can be no greater satisfaction than using a mud kitchen to produce real food! Or at the very least, food for your feathered garden friends. These bird feeders provide a great opportunity to introduce math language into play as you measure ingredients using cups. Using hands and fingers to squish and squash the mixture will not only provide a fun sensory experience, but is great for building hand and finger strength, too.

Supplies

Mixing bowl

Mixing spoon

2 cups (226 g) bird seed

2 cups (225 g) grated cheese

1½ cups (390 g) lard or peanut butter (add more if needed)

Raisins (optional)

Plain peanuts (optional)

Pine cones (2 or 3 for every one feeder)

String

Scissors

How to Make It

In a mixing bowl, stir together the bird seed, cheese and lard. If you're using lard, make sure it's at room temperature so it's soft enough to mix.

Add in a good sprinkling of raisins and peanuts, then use your hands and fingertips to squish the mixture together.

Tie your pine cones together in groups of two or three, looping the string around the top and securing it, and making sure to leave a free length of string to tie to a branch or bird feeder. Pack the bird food mixture onto the pine cones.

Choose a suitable place to put your feeder and watch from afar as your feathered friends enjoy their culinary treat.

Mud Slime

This is a slippery, gooey, stretchy alternative to mud dough. This mud slime uses only three ingredients and will keep the kids occupied for ages.

Supplies

1 (5-oz [147-ml]) bottle Elmer's clear school glue

Mixing bowl

Mixing spoon

Mud (damp or wet)

½ cup (120 ml) liquid starch

How to Make It

Squeeze the entire bottle of glue into a bowl and mix in a few spoonfuls of mud. Make sure the mud you use is moist but not full of water, or the ingredients may not bind well.

Stir in the liquid starch, first using a spoon and then using your hands to combine the ingredients. You will see it quickly start to form into a slime consistency.

Tip it out onto a flat surface and knead until it's no longer sticky. If the slime is still sticky after lots of kneading, add a little more starch.

Squeeze the entire bottle of glue into the bowl.

Add a few spoonfuls of mud and mix.

Stir in the liquid starch.

Afternoon Tea

As an English native, I couldn't resist including a mud kitchen version of classic afternoon tea—with a twist. As with all the imaginative play ideas in this section of the book, role playing in this way will help improve your child's language development and social skills, and will also be lots of fun.

Supplies

Natural loose parts: leaves, petals, acorns, pine cones, pebbles, grass, etc.

Teapot

Water

Wooden spoon

Teacups

Teaspoons

Mud Pies (page 25)

Spatula

Measuring cups

Jugs, bowls, pans, etc.

Serving dishes or trays—bonus points for a cake stand

How to Play

Prepare the "tea" by placing foraged leaves, flowers or grass inside your teapot and add water to "steep." You may choose to use hot (not boiling) water here if you wish, but make sure you closely supervise your child at all times and ensure the water isn't hot enough to scald.

Stir and pour into cups. Pouring in this way is a brilliant activity for improving accuracy and hand-eye coordination. When the "tea" is in the cups, pretend to drink or pour it back into the teapot and start all over again.

Use the Mud Pie recipe to create some wonderful cake creations and adorn them with natural loose parts—flowers, pine cones, pebbles, etc. Serve on a tray or platter.

Why not allow your child to serve you afternoon tea while you play along? Describing how the cakes and tea "taste" will help build your child's vocabulary and understanding of descriptive language. Enjoy as they join in with you.

Tea and Coffee Station

Kids know that mom and dad just love a good cup of tea or coffee, and they will love making their own version to serve to you. This activity is a sensory delight, with both the aroma and the textures of the coffee beans, tea leaves and frothy milk providing a wonderful opportunity for descriptive play.

Supplies

Coffee beans

Mortar and pestle

Jugs, pans, etc.

Warm water

Tea leaves, tea bags or foraged leaves, flowers or grass

Teapot

Mugs

Spoons

Serving tray

Wooden spoon

Measuring cups

Pots and containers for play

FOR THE FROTHY MILK

2 tbsp (30 ml) dish soap

¼ cup (60 ml) water

Bowl

Whisk

How to Play

Prepare the coffee by allowing your child to grind the beans using a mortar and pestle. If you don't have one, use a rock. Not only is this great fun (and smells amazing), but it is a brilliant activity for strengthening shoulders and arms and developing gross motor skills. Add the coffee beans to a pan or jug of warm water and stir.

To make the frothy milk, add the dish soap and water to a bowl and whisk, whisk, whisk until there are stiff peaks in the foam. Scoop it up with a spoon and pour on top of the coffee.

Prepare the tea by placing the tea or foraged items inside your teapot and add water to "steep." You may choose to use hot (not boiling) water here if you wish, but make sure you closely supervise your child at all times and ensure the water isn't hot enough to scald. Stir and pour into the mugs. Pouring in this way is a brilliant activity for improving accuracy and hand-eye coordination. When the tea is in the mugs, pretend to drink it or pour it back into the teapot and start all over again.

Ice Cream Parlor

This simple ice cream sensory role play is the perfect activity for children of all ages. Using a hole punch to create the toppings will provide brilliant hand strength practice (perfect for writing skills), and the option to introduce money to the play makes it the ideal all-around activity.

Supplies

Flowers, leaves and herbs, for the toppings

Hole punch

Small containers or bowls

Dirt and water, or mud

Large bowl

Ice cream scoops

Sundae dishes, bowls or toy ice cream cones

Pots and containers for play

Trinket box (optional)

Coins (optional)

How to Play

Before the little ones start scooping and serving the ice cream, get them going on creating some delicious natural toppings. Use the hole punch on the leaves or petals to make "leaf sprinkles."

Set up the parlor by sorting the toppings into separate bowls or containers and heaping some dirt or mud into a large container with some ice cream scoops nearby. If you choose to use dirt, it may need a little water mixed in to achieve an ice cream texture.

Let your child set about scooping, serving and choosing toppings. They may even want to add in a sprig of lavender or rosemary for a sensory twist on a chocolate stick.

Why not introduce the idea of money into the play? Set up a simple cash register using a compartmentalized box (trinket boxes work well for this) and give your child some coins to sort. Vary the amount of money and types of coins, depending on their age and ability. Together you can decide on the prices for the different ice cream creations. Just make sure you hold some change back so you can pay for your ice cream!

Herb Garden

Creating an herb garden for your mud kitchen will not only provide a brilliant sensory element to your child's play but will also give you the opportunity to teach them about different edible plants and their uses. This activity can easily be completed in 30 minutes, but if you would like to extend the experience, why not take your child to your local garden center and choose the herbs together?

Supplies

Compost or potting soil

Large plant pot or several 2-liter drink bottles (one for each herb)

Rake

Trowel

Herbs

Watering can

Scissors

Gardening gloves (optional)

How to Make It

Add some compost to a large pot and allow your child to rake the top to create a flat surface. Dig a small hole for each of your herb plants and place it in the hole, lightly pressing down around the roots. Water the herbs to encourage them to continue growing in their new home.

Don't have access to a large pot? You can make a simple DIY herb garden using several large 2-liter drink bottles. Cut the tops off the bottles using a sturdy pair of scissors and fill half the base with compost. Plant one of your chosen herbs and then add more compost around the sides until the roots are covered. Gently press down the compost, then water.

Gently remove the herb from its pot.

Plant in the hole you have created, lightly pressing down around the roots.

Water the planted herbs.

Juice Bar

Ditch the dirt for the day and let your little ones turn their mud kitchen into a juice bar with this fun, sweet-smelling sensory role play idea. Why not provide clean utensils and containers for this activity and ramp up the fun by allowing your children to drink their creations—just like the lemonade stands of your day? This is a particular favorite of mine because it smells so good and looks beautiful, too.

Supplies

Lemons, oranges, limes and any other fruit you would like to add

Cutting board

Sharp knife

Large bowl or drink dispenser

Water

Citrus press (optional)

Herbs

Glasses

Large serving spoons or ladle

Pots and containers for play

How to Play

Prepare the fruit by cutting it in halves or quarters. If you have young children, you may want to do this part yourself. However, I am a great believer in supporting children to develop practical life skills and undertake supervised "risky play," so if you wish to do so, you may like to allow your child to cut the fruit themselves. Take the time to demonstrate and explain how to hold the knife safely and watch carefully as your child undertakes this task. You may be pleasantly surprised at their skill level, and they will love being trusted with such a grown-up task.

Fill a large bowl or drink dispenser with water and add your fruit, squeezing as you do so. You may also wish to add in some herbs, like mint or lavender. Tear, squish, crush or throw them in whole.

Set up the serving station with some glasses and a ladle if the juice is in a large bowl. Now the juice is ready to serve.

Hot Chocolate Station

This easy-to-make mud hot chocolate comes with a whipped cream topping. The cream for this activity is made using aquafaba—the liquid from a can of chickpeas. It's an amazing substance for sensory play (and taste-safe too). If you haven't made it before, you really must give it a go. It's so easy to make, and you can even add a few drops of food coloring to the mix, depending on the type of play. For this activity, we will leave it a realistic white color.

Supplies

Mud or dirt

Water

Wooden spoon

Measuring cups

Jugs, bowls, etc.

Saucepan

Mugs

Spoons

Sticks

Serving tray

Scoops, spoons, pots, containers for play

FOR THE "CREAM"

Sieve

1 (15.5-oz [439-g]) can chickpeas packed in water

Mixing bowl

½ tsp cream of tartar

Whisk

Cinnamon stick

How to Play

Set out the supplies and allow your child to start making their muddy hot chocolate by mixing dirt and water to reach their desired consistency. Pour into mugs.

To make the "cream," drain the can of chickpeas, reserving the water in a mixing bowl and setting the chickpeas aside (use them later to make a tasty curry or some homemade hummus). Add the cream of tartar to the chickpea water and whisk until it resembles whipped cream, with stiff peaks. It takes quite a lot of effort, so don't be discouraged if at first it seems like nothing is happening. Keep whisking.

Spoon the "cream" on top of each mug of hot chocolate, and add a cinnamon stick. Finish with a sprinkle of dirt to make it look oh so realistic.

> NOTE: You can use an electric whisk or stand mixer for ease in mixing the "cream," although I do think it takes away some of the fun of allowing your child to make it themselves. All that whisking is brilliant for arm and shoulder strength, too.

Sandwich Bar

These natural mud sandwiches are so easy and quick for your little one to make. Gather a selection of natural loose parts to act as fillings and encourage them to use their imagination to think of what each item might represent. The possibilities are endless.

Supplies

Large leaves

Natural loose parts: grass, seeds, acorns, etc.

Plate

Mud

Butter knife

Scoops, spoons, pots, containers for play

How to Play

Gather some large leaves and natural loose parts from the garden.

Place a large leaf on a plate or flat surface and add a dollop of mud on top, gently spreading it out with a knife. Add some natural loose parts on top of the mud: a sprinkle of grass, a few seeds, even a couple of acorns—it all depends on the type of sandwich your child is making.

Add a second leaf on top to act as the top slice of bread and serve.

Mud Café Menu

Mud pies $2
Mud ice cream $4
Leaf kebabs $3
Leaf sandwiches $5
Muddy hot chocolate $1

Christened

Mud Café

Set the table and press the napkins—it's time for the opening of the Mud Café! Let your little one choose their favorite recipes and activities and pull them all together to make one fantastic mud café. This is not only a brilliant opportunity for imaginative role play, but if your child is old enough, it's a fantastic way to bring math and writing into the game, too.

Supplies

Fabric for table linens

Cutlery

Plates, bowls, cups, etc.

Mud Cookies (page 29), leaf sandwiches (page 50), Mud Pies (page 25), hot chocolate (page 49)—any of your favorites from this chapter

Pad of paper

Pencil

Scoops, spoons, pots, containers for play

Coins

How to Play

Allow your child to set the table using the linens, cutlery and plates. Let them do this independently, but offer help if they ask, guiding them on how to set a table. You may want to discuss what your own dinner table looks like at meal times, or what you find on a table in a café or restaurant.

If you are playing the role of the customer, allow your child to serve you their creations, playing along and acting as if you were in a real café.

Ask to see the menu. Young children can create this independently by making marks and/or writing on their paper. If your child understands phonics and sight words, you can help them write a menu listing the things for sale in their café.

When your visit to the café is over, don't forget to pay. The older your child is, the better understanding they will have on the concept of money, but it is never too early to use the basic concepts as part of play. Stick to simple denominations to make it easy and fun, and use real coins where possible.

Small World Play

Mud kitchen play doesn't always have to revolve around recipes and ingredients. In fact, your mud kitchen will lend itself perfectly to all sorts of imaginative play. I call these "small world" activities because they use small toys and props to enhance play and fantasy.

All of these activities will require a play tray of some sort. This helps to contain the small pieces and provides a focused area of play for your child. You can find big trays like the ones you see in the pictures at many educational supply stores or online stores like Amazon (just search for "play tray" or "tuff tray"). Smaller trays are often easier to use and are much more portable. They are definitely my preferred way to set up role-play activities. You can use a planting tray, an old plastic serving tray or even a fridge organizer. They all work perfectly for messy play and are inexpensive.

These activities are great for both toddlers and much older children—and ideal for cooperative sibling play. If your child is younger, you may want to consider using taste-safe mud (page 14) instead of the real deal.

Diggerland

Grab your excavators and get digging! This is the perfect small world setup for any vehicle-mad little ones. It's a firm favorite in our house, and my son will play with this activity all day long. Just what you need if you have a few things to do around the house.

Supplies

Dirt

Sand

Pebbles and rocks

Play tray

Cereal (save any old cereal rather than buying new, if you can)

Toy diggers, excavators and other vehicles

How to Play

Set up your small world activity by placing the dirt, sand and pebbles into the play tray. You can either add the cereal as it is or crush it before adding. How you add these elements is up to you, but I quite like to put each filler in its own zone—then your child is free to mix them or keep them separate if they desire.

Add a few of your child's favorite toy vehicles.

You can make this even messier by using some mud and providing water, too.

Fantasy Farmyard

This activity is one that has appeal across many ages. Who doesn't love a trip to the farm? Play along with your child, making the sounds of the different animals and introducing new vocabulary: lamb, piglet, dairy, hay bale and so on.

Supplies

Mud

Sawdust

Hay or straw

Grass

Play tray

Toy farm animals

Dish soap

Warm water

Bowl

Scrubbing brush, cloth or sponge

How to Play

Set up your small world activity by placing the mud, sawdust, hay, grass and other fillers into the play tray. You might want to use two trays for this activity: one to act as the field or hay barn, and one to contain the mud.

Add some farm animals and start playing.

When the muddy fun is finished, add a squirt of dish soap to some warm water in a bowl and let your child get to work, scrubbing their animals clean.

Fairy Garden

I don't think I am the only one who would have gone crazy for this as a child. A fairy garden makes a beautiful addition to your garden, and as long as you choose a weather-resistant container, you can even leave it out permanently. If you would prefer to pack your fairy garden away at the end of the day, set it up in a play tray, as you do with the other activities in this chapter. This doesn't just have to be a fairy garden; you could make it into a magical woodland, a dinosaur park or a mini town. So many possibilities!

Supplies

Large container, bucket or planter (or a play tray for a non-permanent version)

Soil or compost

Plants and herbs (whole plants for planting)

Pebbles or glass beads

Sticks, small logs, log slices

Toy fairy figurines

Fairy doors or fairy houses (optional)

NOTE: Check out your local pet or aquarium supply store or garden center for natural-looking "fairy" accessories and additions.

How to Play

Fill a large container with soil until it almost reaches the top.

This is definitely an activity to set up together. Show your child all the items you have gathered and allow them to decide where and how to place things in their fairy garden. When it's their own creation, they will love it even more.

Plant your chosen plants in the soil and then create different areas of the garden, using the pebbles, sticks and logs to separate them. Add any figures and furnishings you like.

Glittery Fairy Mud

This activity is for any little one who likes an added dash of magic (or glitter) in their play. Leave it as basic glittery mud and let your child explore and play as they wish (fairy mud makes great colorful Mud Pies [page 25]), or add some fairy figurines and loose parts for some creative play.

Supplies

Soil or dirt

Water

Mixing bowl

Wooden spoon

Powder paint or grated sidewalk chalk

Glitter

Flowers and/or petals

Glass beads

Sequins

Shells

Toy fairy figurines (optional)

How to Play

Mix together equal parts soil and water in the mixing bowl until you achieve a muddy consistency. Add in the powder paint. Let your child choose the colors and throw in as much or as little as they desire.

Sprinkle and top your creations with glitter and flower petals.

Enhance your fairy mud even more with some loose parts—try glass beads or sequins, shells or even fairy figurines.

Jurassic Swamp

This wonderfully slimy swamp activity is messy, satisfying and taste-safe too. Chia seed slime is one of my go-to messy play activities. It's so ridiculously easy to make, it's got amazing sensory benefits and it's completely safe for even babies to play with. You'll have to mix up the slime a few hours before your child can play with it. That's something you can do together.

Supplies

Chia seeds

Water

Bowl (a cereal bowl will be big enough)

Food coloring (think swamp colors)

Taste-safe mud (page 14)

Play tray

Leaves and grass

Toy swamp creatures: dinosaurs, monsters, insects, etc.

How to Play

To make the swamp slime, mix some chia seeds with water (enough to just cover them in the bowl). Add a few drops of your chosen food coloring and mix again. Leave it in the fridge for a few hours or overnight.

When the slime is ready, add it and the mud to the play tray. Cover with some leaves and grass. You may even want to stick the leaves upright in the mud so they look like trees or mangroves.

Add some swamp creatures and start playing.

Dino Dig

This activity was always a huge hit in my classroom and is one of our favorites at home, too. It's perfect for budding paleontologists and dino-mad little ones. It is also the perfect partner to the DIY Mud Fossils on page 145.

Supplies

Sand

Dirt

Play tray

DIY Mud Fossils (page 145) or toy skeletons and bones

Toy dinosaurs

Clean paintbrushes

Tweezers

Magnifying glass

Basket, bowl or box, to collect your treasures

How to Play

Add a layer of sand and dirt to the bottom of the play tray and then place the fossils and figurines on top. Cover and hide them with the remaining sand and dirt. You may want to arrange a few of them so that they are peeking out from the top of the dirt.

Ask your child to find what is hidden inside. You may like to explain the role of an archaeologist and pretend to dust off and inspect each find using the brushes, tweezers and magnifying glass. Even younger children will enjoy the act of cleaning and dusting off their finds using the paintbrush.

Add each discovery to the basket or bowl until they have all been found. Then rebury them and play again.

Use the tweezers to pick up the fossils.

Your child may enjoy re-hiding the fossils and dinosaurs after they have found them.

Providing brushes and magnifying glasses will make this an "authentic" archaeological dig!

Carrot Dig

There's nothing better than growing your own—but let's face it, sometimes we don't have the time to plant those seeds and wait for the veggies to grow (although I would highly recommend trying that). This activity is quick and easy to set up and will help your little one begin to understand where carrots come from, encourage healthy eating and offer lots of opportunity for great mud play.

Supplies

Deep play tray, plastic bin or plant pots

Compost or soil

Carrots (ideally with the leafy greens still attached)

Trowel and/or spade

Vegetable scrubbing brush

Bowl

Water

Vegetable peeler (optional)

Knife (optional)

How to Play

Half-fill the play tray or pots with compost and add in the carrots, pointed end down, as they would grow naturally. Fill in with the rest of the compost, so that only the tops of the carrots are showing.

Provide your little one with a trowel or a spade and encourage them to get digging and pulling those carrots!

When all the carrots have been uncovered, your child may enjoy replanting them themselves, or decide to be rewarded for their hard work with a snack.

Provide a scrubbing brush and a bowl of clean water to clean the carrots, and then supervise and assist with peeling and chopping, if you'd like.

NOTE: You can use toy versions of the trowel and spade, but I like to use real garden tools, even in play. You can easily find mini, kid-size versions online.

NOTE: Make sure you talk to your child about safely handling the trowel, vegetable peeler and knife; make sure they keep their fingers away from the sharp edges and hold only the handle. Depending on the age of your child, you may want to place your own hands over theirs as they work. Never leave your child unattended with sharp tools.

Seed Planting

Take the play one step further with this activity and allow your child to have a go at seed planting. The best way to offer this activity is to provide all the necessary resources and then let your child play in whatever way they like. You can, of course, be on hand to offer guidance or talk about seed planting and how plants grow. You may also like to set aside an individual plant pot and a few seeds so that you can have one guaranteed plant in a few weeks' time.

Supplies

Deep play tray

Compost or potting soil

Trowel and/or small spade

Seeds (try to choose seeds of different shapes and sizes)

Tray or bowl, to hold the loose seeds

Watering can, water, plant pots for play

How to Play

Fill the deep play tray with compost and lay out the gardening tools and loose seeds to one side.

Allow your little one to explore by digging, mixing, transferring compost and exploring the seeds. While they do so, you can offer comments such as, "Look at the seeds. They are all different colors and shapes." Or, "I wonder what might happen if we push the seed down into the compost and leave it?"

This prompts your little one to think about plants, seeds and growth, while still having fun playing in a child-led way.

NOTES: You can use toy versions of the trowel and spade, but I like to use real garden tools, even in play. You can easily find mini, kid-size versions online.

Mud Art

Expressive arts and the use of mixed media are such important components of an early-years education. These activities will allow your child to explore different arts and crafts techniques, experiment with tools and materials and hone their gross and fine motor skills.

Rainbow Mud

This rainbow mud is so incredibly simple to make, so beautiful to look at and isn't actually mud at all. Clean mud, as it is often called in the play community, uses just soap and toilet paper to make a sensory-rich, gooey mulch, similar in consistency to mud. Use it on its own or combine it with small world play for a magical experience.

Supplies

2 rolls of toilet paper

Water

Grater

1 bar of soap

Play tray or bin

Disposable cups

Poster paint in a variety of colors

Mixing spoon

Scoops, spoons, pots, containers for play

How to Make It

Before you start, soak the two rolls of toilet paper in water until they are sodden.

Grate the entire bar of soap into the play tray and then, using your hands, shred the water-soaked toilet paper on top. Use your hands to squish and mix everything together, until the soap flakes and toilet paper are combined to make the clean mud.

Divide the clean mud into the disposable cups (one cup for each color you are making) and add a squirt of poster paint to each one. Stir with a spoon until the mud reaches the desired color.

This rainbow mud is brilliantly fun to squish, squash, press and mold. It's the perfect way to build your little one's hand strength while providing a great sensory experience, and because it's made from soap, it's really easy to clean up, too.

NOTES: Depending upon the age of your child, you may like to demonstrate how to use the grater first, showing them how to keep their fingers and knuckles out of the way.

If you have a younger child, place your own hands over theirs as you help them.

Chalk Mud Paint

I love activities that are so much fun that little ones have no idea how many brilliant skills they are acquiring. Making and playing with this fun and easy chalk mud paint requires hand strength, fine motor skills and coordination as little ones grate, mix and paint using their hands and fingers.

Supplies

Grater

Sidewalk chalk in a variety of colors

Bowls

Dirt or soil

Water

Paper (optional)

Paintbrushes (optional)

How to Play

Help your child use the grater to grate their chosen color of sidewalk chalk into a small bowl and set it to one side.

Mix together the dirt and water to make mud and then add the chalk powder. Mix together to make the muddy chalk paint.

Chalk paint like this can be used on paper, but our favorite way to play is to paint using brushes or fingers on the sidewalk or back patio. The best part is that when you're all done, it just washes away.

Why not experiment with combining different colors of sidewalk chalk to make different paint colors?

NOTE: Make sure you supervise your child as they use the grater. This can still be done independently, depending on their age, but with some verbal support and a watchful eye to protect little fingers.

Mud Mandalas

Mandalas are having a bit of a moment in the play community, not least because they are beautiful and provide active learning opportunities (math and creativity in particular), but also because creating them allows children to spend time focusing, reflecting and practicing mindfulness. Mindful meditation and play are so important in this fast-paced world of screen time and choice overload, and allowing our children to spend 5 minutes or 50 minutes simply enjoying the process of quiet creation can be so beneficial to their well-being and mental health. Why not join in alongside them? We could all use a positive mental health boost sometimes!

Supplies

Shallow circular dish or tray

Damp mud

Natural loose parts: leaves, petals, acorns, pine cones, pebbles, grass, etc.

Bowls or pots, to hold your loose parts

How to Play

Fill the dish or tray with mud and press it down to create a flat surface.

Collect some natural loose parts or use those you already have in your mud kitchen, and use them to create a beautiful mandala. You might like to show the photograph here to your child as a starting point, or just get to work creating your own and let them play and create alongside you.

Encourage your child to press down gently on each loose part they add, so it doesn't move around as easily.

Mud Creatures

These mud creatures are not only fun to make and provide a great creative outlet, but the process of molding, shaping and squashing the clay is also fantastic for hand and arm strength—the necessary precursor to writing. If you would like to be able to preserve your child's creation, you may want to start out working on a plate, tray or even a wood or stone slab on which to create.

Supplies

Mud or clay

Natural loose parts: sticks, pebbles, leaves, petals, acorns, pine cones, grass, etc.

Bowls or pots, to hold your loose parts

How to Play

Grab a handful or two of mud or clay and mold it into the body of a creature. Be aware that if you would like to save the creation, it would be wise to place this on a portable surface.

When your child is happy with the shape of their creature's body, add features using natural loose parts. Sticks for legs, pebbles for eyes, leaves for scales—the only limit is their imagination.

Leave it in the sun or a warm place to dry out.

NOTE: Mud creatures are often very delicate when dry, so avoid touching them if possible.

Colorful Puddle Splashing

This activity doesn't require a mud kitchen, but it is so popular in our house (and was always a favorite of the children I taught) and is such a brilliant outdoor rainy day activity that I just *had to* include it.

Supplies

Puddles, either created naturally by the rain or using a hose

Jars or cups, to hold each color of paint

Powder paint in various colors

Paintbrushes (optional)

Paper (optional)

How to Play

Wait for a rainy day or use a hose to create some puddles in your backyard or out on the street (they need to be on a paved or hard surface for the best results).

Fill some jars with powder paint and allow your child to tip, pour or sprinkle the colors into the puddles, one at a time. Watch as the colors mingle and mix with the water, turning it into a beautiful colored puddle—perfect for splashing in.

This is the ideal opportunity to introduce the idea of color mixing by adding two or more colors to the puddle and watching what happens. You could even talk about the primary and secondary colors and ask your child to predict what will happen when you mix certain colors together.

Paintbrushes can extend the activity even further, either by painting right onto the ground or on paper.

Natural Mud Art

Who needs paint or paintbrushes? This all-natural way to create art is beautiful and effective. Based upon a well-regarded Forest School activity, this natural twist on the traditional paintbrush has always proved a hit with the children I have taught. The foraging element is as much a part of the activity as the painting itself, and is a brilliant way to connect with nature, as well as making a great prewriting activity and introducing the idea of creating alternative artwork.

Supplies

Basket

Variety of medium or large leaves and flowers

Sticks

String or twine, cut into 12-inch (30-cm) lengths

Scissors

Mud

Water

Paper

How to Make It

Grab a basket and go foraging in your garden or local green space (remembering to only take things that are already on the ground). Look for interesting leaves and sturdy flowers to make the bristles of your brush, gathering bunches of each. Collect sticks to create the handles.

To make the paintbrushes, gather together a selection of leaves and make a bunch (try to use the same type in each bunch). Tie them to the end of a stick using the string, making sure to tie them on securely.

Mix the mud with a small amount of water to make a paint-like consistency. Experiment with different ratios of mud to water and even different types of mud to see how the color and texture can vary.

Dip your natural paintbrushes into the mud and then paint onto the paper, creating a standalone art piece or a background for a more detailed drawing. Why not use the mud art piece as the background for a natural observational line drawing?

Tire Track Art

If my son could pick one project in this entire book to call his favorite, this would be it. It's one of those brilliant activities that takes minutes to set up but engages children for ages. There are so many different ways to extend and change the play, too, from varying the size and type of vehicles to experimenting with mud paint consistency.

Supplies

Large roll of paper

Heavy books, rocks or other objects, to use as weights

Mud

Water

Shallow tray

Toy trucks or other wheeled vehicles with an obvious tread in the tires

How to Play

Lay out the roll of paper along the ground and weigh down the ends.

Make mud paint by mixing mud and water and pouring it onto a shallow tray.

Roll the trucks on the mud and then roll them along the paper roll to make tire tracks. Experiment with using vehicles of different sizes and making patterns on the paper.

Encourage your child to experiment with different consistencies of mud paint by varying the ratio of mud to water and seeing how it affects the tire tracks.

Imagination Stones

Don't buy toy food for your mud kitchen—make your own instead by creating beautiful painted stones! This is a really lovely activity to work on together. Not only is creating your own play food super cost-effective, but it gives your child the opportunity to plan out and create exactly what they need for play. It's a great way to talk about food groups and healthy eating, too.

Supplies

Flat river rocks or large pebbles

Acrylic paint

Paintbrushes

Pictures of food, to use as inspiration (optional)

Paper (optional)

Pencils (optional)

Clear varnish, clear coat spray paint or clear nail polish

How to Play

Wash and dry your rocks before painting.

Choose the type of food you would like to represent and paint the design onto the rock—you may wish to draw it out onto a piece of paper first so you know what you are aiming for.

When the paint is dry, cover the whole rock with a layer of clear varnish to seal and protect the design. If you are using a clear coat spray paint, make sure you do this step in a well-ventilated area (outdoors is best) and away from children.

Forest Faces

These wonderfully earthy faces are made from salt dough and natural objects, using a tree trunk as your easel. They are a Forest School classic, and for good reason. They are so simple to make and allow imaginations and creativity to run wild. You could choose to make human faces, monster faces or even animals.

Supplies

2 cups (250 g) all-purpose flour

1 cup (292 g) salt

Mixing bowl

1 cup (240 ml) water

Natural loose parts

How to Make It

Mix the flour and salt together in a bowl and then slowly add the water a few spoonfuls at a time. Mix together with your hands until the dough is smooth and easy to handle. Tip out the dough and knead for roughly 10 minutes until it is no longer sticky.

Press a ball of salt dough firmly onto the trunk of a tree, then pull it away. Decorate the imprinted pattern by pushing loose parts into or onto the dough to make a face. You could even make imprints or patterns by pressing the loose parts onto the sculpture and then removing them.

You could use leaves for hair, seed pods for eyes, a stick for a nose . . . the only limit is your imagination!

NOTES: This recipe is for salt dough, but alternatively, you could use natural clay.

If you would like to bake your salt dough creation to harden it (perfect for making ornaments), preheat the oven to 250°F (120°C) and bake for around 2 hours until it's dry and hard.

Nature Stones

These nature stones make beautiful decorations or items to enhance other activities. I like to use air-dry modeling clay (the type that doesn't need kiln firing) from our local craft store, but if you have clay soil, you may wish to use that instead.

Supplies

Clay (natural or modeling)

Natural textured loose parts: veined leaves, nuts, seed heads, pine cones, etc.

Clear varnish or clear coat spray paint

How to Play

Take a handful of clay, roll it into a ball and then press down on the top to make a disc about 2 inches (5 cm) thick.

Select one of the natural loose parts and press it into the top of the disc, pulling it away to leave an imprint.

Cover the finished nature stone with a layer of clear varnish to protect the design. If you are using a clear coat spray paint, make sure you do this step in a well-ventilated area (outdoors is best) and away from children.

Clay Faces

These clay faces are so much fun to make, and if you use air-dry clay, your child will have a fantastic keepsake. Providing your child with a mirror will mean they can base their sculpture on their own face, and it will give you the perfect opportunity to talk about facial features and compare your faces.

Supplies

Clay (natural or modeling)

Mirror

Water

Acrylic paint (optional)

Paintbrushes (optional)

Clear varnish or clear coat spray paint

How to Play

Give your child a ball of clay, either straight from your garden if you have clay-based soil, or modeling clay. Encourage them to flatten it down and mold the sides to represent the shape of their face (or the face they are creating).

Give them another piece of clay from which to make the features. Encourage them to look in the mirror and talk together about their facial features, looking at their size and shape. Stick these down onto the face by using your finger to apply a little water to each feature and placing it in the correct position, pressing down to secure.

If you would like to keep the sculpture, leave it to dry.

Once dry, you may choose to paint the finished sculpture. Apply a layer of clear varnish after painting, or before if you are leaving the face its natural color. If you are using a clear coat spray paint, make sure you do this step in a well-ventilated area (outdoors is best) and away from children.

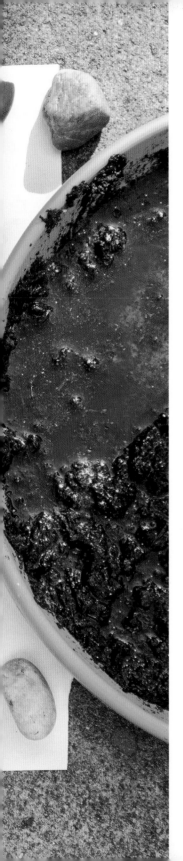

Messy Games

These messy games incorporate more traditional learning opportunities, such as numbers and letters, alongside muddy team games and family fun. Old clothes and hoses at the ready—it's about to get messy!

Shape Play

Mud play is a great way to introduce math skills, and this shape activity
is no exception. Play alongside your child for this one and you will probably
find that next time they are playing in the mud independently,
they'll pick up where you left off.

Supplies

Mud

Natural loose parts

How to Play

Find a flat surface to work on and shape and mold the mud into
different 2D shapes. Work alongside your child and create the
shapes together, talking about the number of sides and corners
as you go.

When you have made all the 2D shapes on the list, decorate them
using your collection of natural loose parts.

- Triangle
- Circle
- Square
- Rectangle
- Diamond
- Oval
- Heart
- Pentagon
- Hexagon
- Octagon

Hidden Letters

Your little one will love playing pirate and discovering the buried letters in this fun activity. What's more, there are so many additional learning opportunities and ways to play. Check out the game suggestions for some ideas.

Supplies

Deep play tray

Soil or compost

Waterproof alphabet letters

Spade

Bucket

NOTE: Foam bath letters are my favorite for this activity, but any waterproof letters will do.

How to Play

Fill the play tray half full with dry soil and place the letters on top, covering them with the rest of the soil so that they are hidden. (You might want to leave a few peeking out so it looks enticing.)

Let your child have fun digging out and finding the letters to put into their bucket.

If you would like to extend the learning further, why not play one of these letter games?

Take turns pulling a letter out of the soil and say the name it has in the alphabet. When all the letters have been pulled out, arrange them along the ground in alphabetical order and then sing the alphabet song.

Take turns pulling a letter out of the soil, but this time say its phonics sound. When all the letters have been pulled out, lay the letters on the ground and say a sound, then ask your child to find the corresponding letter. Trade places and let them say a sound for you to find, too; they will love being the "teacher."

When all the letters have been pulled out of the soil, ask your child to rebury them one at a time. Say the letter's name or sound so they know which one to bury next.

Hidden Numbers

This hidden numbers game combines math and motor skills as little ones uncover the buried treasure and clean it off using a squirt bottle. Bottles like these are brilliant for developing hand strength, and children absolutely love using them to spray everything in sight.

Supplies

Deep play tray

Mud

Waterproof numbers

Spade

Spray bottle filled with water

Bucket

How to Play

Fill the play tray half full with wet mud and place the numbers on top, covering them with the rest of the mud so that they are hidden. (You might want to leave a few peeking out so it looks enticing.)

Let your child have fun digging out and finding the numbers. Reveal the number covered in mud by using the spray bottle to spritz it and clean it, and then put it in their bucket.

If you would like to extend the learning further, why not play one of these number games?

Take turns pulling a number out of the mud and saying what it is. When all the numbers have been pulled out, arrange them along the ground in numerical order.

With the numbers on the ground in the correct order, ask your child to point to a certain number as you call out its name. Make this game harder by mixing up the numbers so they aren't in order.

Lay out all the numbers on the ground so they are mixed up. With your child holding the spray bottle, call out a number and ask them to spray the correct number.

NOTE: Foam bath numbers are my favorite for this activity, but any waterproof numbers will do.

Muddy River

If you have a whole morning or afternoon to fill, this is the activity for you.
I have never known something so simple to elicit such squeals of delight
from children of all ages—and to be honest, it's easy to see why. This is a
great way to introduce the concept of floating and sinking, and
the power of water as it moves all in its path.

Supplies

Heavy duty aluminum foil

Rocks or pebbles

Bucket

Hose or jugs of water

Mud, soil or dirt (optional)

Natural loose parts (optional)

Toy boats (optional)

How to Play

Create the river by pulling out a piece of foil to the desired length
(depending on how long or short you would like the river to be)
and folding it in half lengthwise. It is not absolutely necessary to
fold the foil in half, but I find this makes it a little more sturdy
and robust.

Set the foil river down onto the grass or patio. This does work a
little better if it is on a slight incline, but don't worry if you only
have flat ground to work with. Place some rocks or pebbles at
intervals along the river to stop the foil from blowing away.

Put a bucket at one end (to catch the water so it doesn't go to
waste) and then place a hose at the other end—the water source.
If you don't have a hose, pouring jugs full of water down the river
will work just as well.

Add some mud, soil or dirt into your river to make the water
muddy and watch it slowly wind its way along. You may also want
to add some natural loose parts, or even toy boats, and observe
how the water moves them along.

Why not create two rivers side by side and have a race?

Mud Ball Fight

Forget snowball fights—the mud ball fight is where it's at!
This one is guaranteed to get super messy, but it's so much fun.
So embrace the dirt and get ready to laugh!

Supplies

Old clothes
Mud (and lots of it!)

How to Play

Before you start, make sure you and your children are dressed for mess, in clothes you don't mind getting very dirty.

Create a collection of mud balls by scooping and molding mud into small round shapes. The best kind of mud to use is from sticky, clay-based soil or it won't hold together very well. If you are using mud straight from the ground, check that it doesn't contain any rocks or pebbles.

You can either throw the mud balls at a target (this is best with younger children) or divide into two teams and throw the mud balls at each other. You may wish to decide the rules of the game first, and I suggest a below-the-waist-only rule is a good idea.

Mud Bath

There's nothing more wonderful or carefree than taking a bath in mud. While the thought of your child being covered head to toe in mud might make you shudder, you may like to know that messy play is actually extremely important for your child's development. It not only provides a tactile sensory experience, but also allows children to develop their language, curiosity and creativity.

Supplies

Old clothes or an all-in-one waterproof playsuit

Large play tray

Mud

Spray bottles filled with water

Hose (optional)

Rain boots (optional)

Pots and pans

Spoons and ladles

Bowls

How to Play

Before you start, make sure you and your children are dressed for mess, in clothes you don't mind getting very dirty. Fill your large play tray with a layer of wet mud, to act as the bath, and set up some spray bottles filled with water nearby. You may also like to turn on the hose to make it extra messy (and to clean off afterward).

Encourage your children to dive in! They can squelch, wiggle and scoop the mud, using their hands, feet and tools too. While the children are playing, be aware that the play tray and wet mud can become quite slippery, so sitting rather than standing is advised. Grab some of the utensils, pots and pans from your mud kitchen for added fun with scooping, stirring and pouring.

Your child will love adding water to their mud bath using a hose pipe or buckets of water!

Encourage your child to think about how the mud feels under their hands and feet!

Skin-Safe Mud Mask

This skin-safe mud mask uses an alternative to my taste-safe mud
(page 14) and is actually great for skin, as well as being fun to play with.
Why not teach your child about the history of using mud masks as you play
and paint each other's faces?

Supplies

Half a banana

Potato masher

Mixing bowl

1 tsp cocoa powder

2 to 3 tbsp (30 to 45 ml) Greek
or plain yogurt

Wide paintbrush (an unused
foundation brush works well)

How to Make It

Mash the banana in the bowl and mix in the cocoa powder
and yogurt.

Test the mask on the skin on the inside of your child's arm, just
above their wrist, to make sure they do not have a reaction. Wait
a few minutes.

Use a wide paintbrush to paint the mixture onto each other's
faces, avoiding the eyes and nostrils.

Relax with your mud masks, or use a camera to take some
silly selfies.

NOTE: Mud masks and mud baths have been used all over the
world for hundreds of years. The Greeks and Romans loved to
bathe in mud and apply it to their faces, and believed it could
even soothe aches and pains. Even today, lots of people believe
that mud is great for skin and leaves it soft and healthy. Does
your skin feel different after the mud mask?

Farm Animal Wash

Looking for a quick activity to set up in under five minutes? Grab some muddy toys, fill a bowl with bubbly water and let the kids get scrubbing. I like to use baby bath wash or shampoo in the water, as it's a bit kinder to eyes and skin than using dish soap.

Supplies

Large play tray

Farm animals or other toys

Mud

Bowl

Water

Baby bath wash or shampoo

Scrubbing brushes, cloths and sponges

How to Play

Set up the play tray with the muddy animals.

Provide a bowl of bubbly water and some sponges, cloths or scrubbing brushes and leave the kids to play.

NOTE: We often use taste-safe mud when we are playing this game. See page 14 for details on how to make your own.

Clay Play

Playing with clay is one of the underpinning activities of the Reggio Emilia Approach to education—an approach developed in Italy almost 100 years ago and one of the leading philosophies of early childhood education across the world. It not only allows your child to express their creativity and develop essential motor skills, but it provides a physical, tangible connection with the Earth.

Supplies

Clay

Flat surface on which to work (I recommend a wooden board)

Water

Natural loose parts

Tools: cutlery, sharp stick, rolling pin, cookie cutters, etc.

Damp cloth to preserve the clay

NOTE: You may wonder, what's so special about clay? Why not just use playdough? While they do serve similar purposes, clay is very different in one important sense—it comes from the Earth. It is cool to the touch, soft on the skin and has a satisfying earthy smell. What's more, just cover it over with a damp cloth after play and you can return to it day after day.

How to Play

Here are some ways to introduce play with clay. These ideas get progressively more challenging, but your child can start at any point and doesn't need to work their way down the list in a linear fashion.

- Poke the clay.
- Lift the clay and feel its weight.
- Scrape the clay with your fingers.
- Pinch it.
- Twist it.
- Press your whole hand into it and then press each finger in turn—which is the most difficult?
- Add water and experiment with what happens.
- Press natural loose parts into the clay to make patterns.
- Roll the clay or squash it flat, making different 2D and 3D shapes.
- Sculpt the clay into a representation of an object.
- Use tools to mark, shape and change the clay.

Making Marks

Making marks can refer to anything from creating small scribbles, lines or circles to drawing pictures or writing words. The types of marks children will make depend on their individual age, ability and preferences, and no one type of mark should be held in higher regard than another. Making marks helps to develop coordination and physical motor skills, as well as creativity, literacy and math, depending on how the child chooses to play.

Supplies

Roll of paper

Pots or bowls, to hold the mud paint

Mud

Water

Paintbrushes of different sizes (wallpaper pasting brushes make great large-scale tools)

Natural paintbrushes (page 85)

Natural loose parts: sticks, twigs, leaves, acorns, pebbles, etc.

Sticks, twigs and branches

How to Play

Lay the roll of paper down along the ground.

Provide a couple of pots or bowls containing mud paint (mud mixed with water). You may like to vary the consistency of the paint in each bowl by changing the ratio of mud to water.

Leave out a selection of brushes, natural paintbrushes (page 85) and loose parts.

Encourage your child to dip the tools into the mud paint and make marks on the paper. They may like to use the natural loose parts to make prints, while the sticks and twigs can be used to drag or roll mud across the surface of the paper.

You can change or adapt this activity by pinning the paper up on a fence or vertical surface. Or get rid of the paper altogether and make marks straight onto the ground or on garden walls.

Handprints and Footprints

This is a great activity for all ages and a really fun idea for some family bonding time. Why not save your masterpiece and display it in a frame?

Supplies

Mud

Water

Mixing bowl

Flat tray

Roll of paper

How to Play

Mix the mud and water to make a mud paint. If you want to keep the prints, make sure your paint is of a thicker consistency.

Put the mud paint into a shallow tray and press in hands and feet (one set at a time is best). Create handprints and footprints by pressing onto the paper. Footprints can easily be created by walking across the paper. This is a great opportunity to talk about why the prints become fainter the farther you walk.

Why not challenge your child to write everyone's name under their individual prints so that you can remember whose is whose?

Let your child paint their own hands and enjoy the sensory experience.

This activity is suitable for all family members!

Mud under bare hands and feet will provide a multi-sensory experience.

Animal Tracks

Animal tracks are imprints that are left behind in soil, snow or mud when an animal walks there. These tracks are used by scientists to identify animals living in a particular area, and by hunters tracking their prey. This activity is an easy way to introduce the idea of animal tracks to your child and talk about the different animals found across the globe.

Supplies

Mud paint (mud mixed with water)

Play tray

Toy animals

Roll of paper (optional)

How to Play

Add the mud paint to the play tray.

Choose an animal toy and dip their feet into the mud paint. Walk the animal across the paper or on soft ground and watch as the tracks appear.

Why not use this as an opportunity to talk about the different footprints animals have? Do the toy animals have accurate tracks? What could you do to alter the footprint so it looks correct?

Change this activity by filling your play tray with thick, compacted mud and walking the animals across the tray to make tracks on the mud's surface.

Time to Clean Up!

Teaching your child to clean up after play is an important practical life skill. While the beauty of a mud kitchen is that items can often be left out in the open and don't require regular cleaning, you may like to gather all the utensils, pots and pans and give them a good scrub every once in a while. In reality, kids love this activity because it provides them with more messy fun and they get to play at being a grown-up.

Supplies

Baby bath wash, shampoo or dish soap

Washing-up bowl

Warm water

Messy mud kitchen items

Scrubbing brushes, cloths and sponges

Old dish towels

How to Play

Create the bubbly water by adding baby bath wash or shampoo to a bowl of warm water. You can also use dish soap if you prefer, but it is a little harsher on skin and eyes.

Give your child a pile of dirty items to clean and let them get into it.

When the items have been cleaned, lay them out on top of the old dish towels to air dry.

Muddy STEM Play

STEM stands for science, technology, engineering and math. It's more than just the teaching of those subjects, though—STEM learning involves the amalgamation of all four subjects into real-world scenarios and experiments. Giving our children access to STEM learning and activities means they will become more creative, better at problem solving and ultimately more ready for the real world as adults.

From creativity and critical thinking to making observations and recording results—the STEM activities in this chapter will allow your child to access mud kitchen play on a whole new level.

Mud Investigation

Become a scientist and explore the properties of mud and dirt! Your child will love learning how to use various tools to explore and make observations in this simple science experiment. Although the activities in this chapter can be tackled in any order, this is a good place to start, as your child will be able to use what they learn to aid them in the other projects.

Supplies

Shallow tray

White paper, to line the tray

Spoons or spades

Sieve

Magnifying glass

Tweezers

Containers with lids for collecting the dirt (recycled plastic food tubs work well)

Sticky labels

Pen or pencil

How to Play

Take your child into your garden or to a local green space and look for different types of mud and dirt. Have a look at the Dirt List for examples of what you might find.

When you have found some dirt, help your child scoop some out and put it into the tray you have lined with paper (the white paper will help you see the details of the dirt more clearly). Talk about what you notice and ask questions as you explore together: "What does it feel like?" "What does it smell like?" "Is the dirt dry, damp or wet?" "Can you see any things (leaves, berries, twigs) in the dirt?" "I wonder if we can find any creatures in the dirt?"

Allow your child time to dig, scoop, sieve, mix and explore. They may like to look more closely using their magnifying glass, or pick up certain elements using their tweezers.

When you have finished, put the dirt sample (checking there are no worms or other mini bugs) into the lidded container and write a label together, saying where you collected the sample.

Move around your garden or local outdoor spaces, collecting dirt samples to build the collection.

Depending on the age of your child, you may wish to consider keeping a journal of your findings with photographs, drawings and notes about your discoveries. You could even put a little dirt into a small plastic bag and staple it to each page.

Dirt List

- Topsoil: the first 2 to 8 inches (5 to 20 cm) of soil—quite literally, the top layer of soil
- Black dirt: rich black or dark brown soil, much like compost
- Chalk soil: contains larger pieces of grit, gravel and rocks
- Silt soil: feels soft, slippery and wet
- Sandy soil: feels gritty and much like sand
- Clay dirt: feels lumpy; it is sticky when wet and extremely hard when dry
- Leaf litter dirt: normally collected under a tree and rich in leaves, twigs and creepy crawlies

DIY Mud Bricks

Fancy making real mud bricks? This is the activity for you! This experiment will allow your child to test different combinations of mud, dirt and natural objects to see which make the best mud bricks. It's a lesson in trial and error with exciting results.

Supplies

Various dirt samples (see Mud Investigation, page 126)

Sand

Dried leaves or grass

Small twigs, to add to the mixture (optional)

Water

Bowls

Spoons

Silicone ice cube tray

How to Play

Mix several different types of dirt together, creating different mixtures to test. Make sure that at least one of the mixtures contains some sand and another contains small pieces of leaves and grass, or small pieces of broken twigs.

Add water to each mixture and combine well, and then scoop small amounts into an ice cube tray. You may wish to use different ice cube trays for each mixture. Press the mixture down into each section of the tray so that it compacts. Talk about what you are doing and ask your child to predict which mixture they think will make the strongest bricks. Gently pop the bricks out of the ice cube tray. You may like to give them a final squeeze to make sure they are fully compacted.

Leave the bricks to dry in the sun for a few days, or you can bake them in the oven on a low temperature (150°F [65°C]) until they are dry and hard, usually a few hours.

You're ready to build! Check out the Mud Houses project on page 133 for some ideas.

> NOTE: It really is important to use a silicone tray for this step, or an ice cube tray with removable dividers, or else the bricks will break as you pop them out.

Mud Castles

This is an alternative to the classic sandcastle. It's a lot messier, but no trip to the beach is required. Depending on your child's preference, you could use loose parts to decorate your castles, or simply smash them down and start again (this is the order of the day at our house).

Supplies

Mud

Water

Sand

Bucket

Straw, grass or leaves

Sandcastle mold

Spade

Natural loose parts, for decoration

How to Play

Create a solid mud castle mixture by combining mud, water and sand in a bucket and mixing it with your hands. Throw in some straw, grass or leaves to act as a binder and mix.

Scoop out some of the mixture and add it to the mold, just as you would if you were building a sandcastle. Pat it down firmly with the spade so that it compacts. When the mold is full, quickly flip it onto a flat surface and pat the top to release the mud castle. Gently lift the mold to reveal the creation underneath and then decorate with loose parts.

Mud Houses

This activity lets children live their building fantasies by using "real" mortar and bricks. There really is no limit to creativity with this project, whether they are building tiny houses for fairies or a large castle or tall tower. To do this project, you will first need to make your own Mud Bricks. Have a look at page 129 to see how.

Supplies

Mud

Water

Mixing bowl

Mud Bricks (page 129)

Spoon or knife (a blunt butter knife works well)

Small sticks

Natural loose parts, for decoration

How to Play

Combine the mud and water in the mixing bowl to make a thick, wet mortar mixture with which to cement the bricks.

Start building a structure, using the mortar to join the mud bricks together. Spread out the mortar with a spoon or a small knife. If you would like to build an opening, use a small stick to bridge the gap and act as a support, and then continue to build on top of it.

Add a roof and other decorations or embellishments using natural loose parts.

Why not experiment with building a tower and seeing how tall you can make it before it falls down?

Rivers, Streams and Dams

This activity needs very little prior planning and you will likely have all you need at home, even if you don't already have your mud kitchen set up. Kids absolutely love water play—something about the way water moves fascinates them—so this activity is guaranteed to create a fun and long-lasting afternoon of play.

Supplies

Spades and scoops

Mud patch in the garden or a large, deep tray filled with mud

Trash can liners (optional)

Hose or jugs of water

Large river pebbles or rocks

How to Play

Use the spades and scoops to dig down into the mud patch to create water courses. Press and compact the sides of the trenches using the flat side of the spade or your hands.

Experiment with creating water courses of different widths and lengths, and join them together to create a river network. You may like to line the trenches with trash can liners if you feel your soil will absorb the water too quickly.

Place a hose at the mouth of the river and turn it on so that the water flows at a medium speed. Not too fast or the courses will be blasted away! If you don't have access to a hose, pouring water from a jug will have the same effect.

Children can use pebbles and rocks to block the flow of water and create a dam, or to redirect the flow of water.

Discuss what happens to the water as it flows through the river system (it is absorbed back into the earth). Experiment with lining the trenches with pieces of plastic and observe the difference it makes.

Mini Beast Hunt

It's important for kids to understand that mud and dirt is not just for play or planting flowers, but that it provides a home to many different creatures. Going on a mini beast hunt, whether in your own garden or in a local park or woodland, will provide a brilliant opportunity for children to learn about the world around them. It will encourage them to use their observation skills, and it gives them a chance to get hands-on with wildlife. The very best time to go mini beast hunting is after it rains.

Supplies

Binoculars

Spade

White sheet of paper

Spoon

Lidded pots or containers (magnifying pots are brilliant if you have one)

Magnifying glass

Insect reference book or your phone

Notepad (optional)

Pencil (optional)

NOTE: If you don't like creepy crawlies, try not to let your dislike show as you look at them together. Take lidded containers and a spade with you, and you can avoid having to touch anything you don't want to.

How to Play

Mini beasts and insects live in all sorts of places around the garden. Some may be found on or in the mud, while others live nearby. Start by looking in dark, damp spots and use these ideas to help track them down—you could even use binoculars to find them from far away.

Gently move and dig down into the soil, turning it over to reveal what is underneath. Carefully lift and look under large stones or logs. Look inside the cracks on the trunk of a tree. Look closely at leaves, particularly the underside (this is a great place to discover caterpillars and ladybugs). Place a white sheet of paper under a tree or bush and gently shake the branches. You will be surprised at what falls out.

Look closely at your discoveries by gently scooping them up using a spoon or leaf and placing them into a container. Use a magnifying glass to look at details and try to decide what you have found. You may like to use a reference book or even your phone to learn more about the creatures you find.

Remember—bugs are very tiny, so be careful if you pick them up and always put them back where you found them.

You may like to encourage your child to keep a record of what you find by drawing a picture of each beast and labeling it.

DIY Worm Farm

Adopt worms for a week with this really simple DIY worm farm.
Watch as they tunnel, creating worm tubes and casts. This is a great activity
for budding biologists, encouraging children to connect with nature and
spend time outdoors. It also helps to develop language and communication
skills, mathematical understanding and scientific inquiry—all
fundamental elements of mud kitchen play.

Supplies

Large plastic drink bottle or deep transparent bin

Scissors (if using a plastic bottle)

Soil

Compost

Sand

Spade or trowel

Worms from the garden

Dark piece of fabric or dark garbage bag

Spray bottle filled with water

NOTES: Refrigerator organizers work well for this activity. No need to feed the worms in your farm; they live off the organic matter and microorganisms in the soil.

How to Make It

If you're using a plastic bottle, cut off the top. Then fill your bottle or bin by putting in layers of soil, compost and sand, in any order you like. The difference in color and texture will really help to show the movement of the worms as they tunnel through your worm farm. Finish off with a top layer of soil, and then you are ready to add your worms.

To find and collect the worms, gently turn over the soil in your garden using a spade or trowel. If the soil is very dry, you may find that lightly hosing it will encourage the worms to appear. When you find a worm, gently place it on top of the soil in your wormery and watch it tunnel down.

To maintain your wormery, loosely cover it with a dark piece of fabric or a dark garbage bag. Keep the soil nice and damp by spraying it with water every few days.

Make sure you gently return the worms to your garden after a week.

Why not seize the opportunity to learn even more about worms and their life cycle? Help your child create a log book, showing drawings or photographs of the wormery, along with their observations.

Fizzing Wizards' Brew

Channel your wizarding skills, turn your mud kitchen into a magical kitchen and mix up this marvelous, colorful, fizzing wizards' brew. No mud required, but it can be added for extra fun and experimentation purposes.

Supplies

Bowl or pan, to act as a cauldron

Vinegar

Powder paint, grated chalk or food coloring

Dish soap

Baking soda

Spoon or stick, to use as a magic wand

Large tray or dish, to catch the overflow (optional)

How to Make It

Fill the cauldron halfway with vinegar and add the coloring of your choice. Several colors together often work to create an extra magical potion.

Add a large squeeze of dish soap (how much depends on the size of your cauldron, but this is a good opportunity to test and experiment). Add in a couple of spoonfuls of baking soda and use the magic wand to stir.

When your potion has finished bubbling and fizzing, simply add more vinegar, baking soda and dish soap to the existing mixture in the bowl and keep stirring.

Why not experiment with adding in different colors to see how they combine?

Mud Volcano

Baking soda and vinegar experiments have long been a favorite of children everywhere. This fun twist means you can build a semi-permanent erupting volcano for fizzing, erupting fun over and over again.

. . . .

Supplies

Empty plastic bottle

Play tray (optional)

Mud

Food coloring (red, orange or yellow)

2 cups (480 ml) vinegar

Bowl

Funnel

1 tbsp (14 g) baking soda

How to Make It

Place the empty bottle onto the soil (or in the play tray if you prefer) and build up the wet mud and dirt around it until it resembles a volcano. Try to cover the top of the bottle so that you can't see it poking out the top.

Mix the food coloring and vinegar in a bowl. Use the funnel to first add the baking soda to the bottle and then the vinegar mixture.

Stand back and watch the volcano erupt! To repeat the experiment, simply add more baking soda and vinegar to the bottle.

Experiment with different ratios of baking soda and vinegar and see how it affects the level of eruption.

DIY Mud Fossils

These mud fossils are easy to make and they look so real. They make great ornaments or loose parts for play. One of our favorite ways to use them is in an archaeological dig small world setup (see page 67 for inspiration).

Supplies

2 cups (250 g) flour

½ cup (146 g) salt

2 tbsp (20 g) cream of tartar

2 tbsp (30 ml) vegetable oil (you can also use baby oil or coconut oil)

Wooden spoon

Mixing bowls

Brown food coloring

1½ cups (360 ml) boiling water

Sand

Loose parts to make the fossil imprints (try thick-veined leaves, feathers, seed pods), or small world toys like dinosaurs

How to Make It

Make the dough by stirring together the flour, salt, cream of tartar and oil in a bowl until they're combined.

In another bowl, add drops of the food coloring to the boiling water until you have the color you want. Add the water to the dry ingredients and combine.

Allow it to cool before taking it out of the bowl and kneading the mixture for several minutes until it is no longer sticky.

Add some of the sand to the dough and knead it in, adjusting the amount to your liking. If the mixture is still sticky, you may want to add a little more sand.

Divide the dough and roll it into small balls. Flatten each one to get a disc. You can adjust the thickness of the disc depending on how thick you would like your fossil to be.

Press your chosen loose part or toy into the dough to make an imprint, and carefully lift it away.

When all your fossils have been created, leave them out in the sun for a couple of days until dry, or place them in the oven for a few hours on a low heat (around 150°F [65°C]) until they're hard and dry.

When your fossils are ready, why not try the Dino Dig on page 67?

Acknowledgments

To my wonderful husband, Lawrence, who worked tirelessly to support us all when I was trying to figure out how to combine my work and home life passions. Thank you for bringing me endless treats, taking the boys so I could have a few hours of quiet in which to write, and for being my all-around rock.

To my boys, Finley and Rupert. I love you both more than words could ever say. You challenge me daily to be the best person I can be and you have both truly changed my life for the better. You won't remember the hours you sat on my knee as I typed one-handed, you pressing laptop keys with sticky fingers and squeezing in quick cuddles between chapters. You won't remember, but just know, your words are in here too—deleted and adjusted though they may be.

To my parents, who gave me the very best childhood anyone could ever ask for. Who sacrificed so much to make sure I was happy and made me into the person I am today. You taught me drive, determination and ambition. Thank you for always answering the phone, even when it's the fifth time in one day. Thank you for your unwavering support and guidance.

To Mandy, our Mary Poppins. I couldn't have written this book without your support and care, not just for our boys but for our whole family.

A huge thank-you to the team at Page Street Publishing for believing in me and supporting me in what is definitely my greatest endeavor thus far.

Finally, to my wonderful community on Instagram, Facebook and YouTube, I honestly can't explain in words how much you all mean to me. Thank you all for your support, your kind words and messages.

Thank YOU for buying this book! I hope that I have helped you to discover the joy I find every day in play.

About the Author

Sophie Pickles is an early years expert and qualified teacher with more than fourteen years of experience working with children. She is passionate about learning outdoors and the benefits it brings to children and adults alike.

Sophie has worked with children from birth to eleven, from Italy and France to the UK, working as a nanny, teacher, educational advisor and parenting coach. She shares her creative ideas for everyday play and advice for parents of babies and toddlers on her Instagram and YouTube platforms, and writes and consults for many leading educational companies and brands.

Sophie lives in the English countryside with her husband, their two lively sons and three lazy cats. Home is a happy place of muddy boots, homemade toys and delighted giggles, where chaos and calm exist in equal measure.

Index